19.75

D0753640

Simms Library
Albuquerque Academy
6400 Wyoming Blvd. N.E.
Albuquerque, NM 87109

6/04

THE HISPANIC INFLUENCE IN THE UNITED STATES

LATINOS
IN AMERICAN HISTORY

LORENZO DE ZAVALA

BY KATHLEEN TRACY

Mitchell Lane
PUBLISHERS

P.O. Box 619
Bear, Delaware 19701

THE HISPANIC INFLUENCE IN THE UNITED STATES

LATINOS
IN AMERICAN HISTORY

OTHER TITLES IN THE SERIES

Visit us on the web: www.mitchelllane.com
Comments? email us: mitchelllane@mitchelllane.com

921
ZAVALA
2003

THE HISPANIC INFLUENCE IN THE UNITED STATES

LATIN❓S
IN AMERICAN HISTORY

LORENZO DE
ZAVALA

BY KATHLEEN TRACY

Mitchell Lane
PUBLISHERS

Copyright © 2003 by Mitchell Lane Publishers, Inc. All rights reserved. No part of this book may be reproduced without written permission from the publisher. Printed and bound in the United States of America.

Printing   1   2   3   4   5   6   7   8

Library of Congress Cataloging-in-Publication Data
Tracy, Kathleen.
    Lorenzo de Zavala / Kathleen Tracy.
        p. cm. — (Latinos in American history)
    Summary: A biography of Lorenzo de Zavala, the statesman who became vice president of the Republic of Texas in 1836.
    Includes bibliographical references (p.) and index.
    ISBN 1-58415-154-4 (lib bdg.)
    1. Zavala, Lorenzo de, 1788-1836. 2. Vice-Presidents—Texas—Biography. 3. Statesmen—Texas—Biography. 4. Texas—History—Republic, 1836-1846. [1. Zavala, Lorenzo de, 1788-1836. 2.Vice-Presidents—Texas. 3. Statesmen. 4. Texas—History—Republic, 1836-1846.] I. Title. II. Series.
    F390.Z4 T74 2002
    976.4'04'092—dc21   2002008334

ABOUT THE AUTHOR: Kathleen Tracy has been a journalist for over twenty years. Her writing has been featured in magazines including The Toronto Star's "Star Week," *A&E Biography* magazine, *KidScreen* and *TV Times*. She is also the author of numerous biographies including "The Boy Who Would Be King" (Dutton), "Jerry Seinfeld - The Entire Domain" (Carol Publishing), "Don Imus - America's Cowboy" (Carroll & Graf), "Mariano Guadalupe Vallejo," and "William Hewlett: Pioneer of the Computer Age," both for Mitchell Lane. She recently completed "God's Will?" for Sourcebooks.

PHOTO CREDITS: Cover: Center for American History; pp. 6, 10 Hulton/Archive; pp. 11, 12 Bettmann/Corbis; p. 13 Barbara Marvis; p. 14 Center for American History; p. 18 Charles & Josette Lenars/Corbis; p. 20 Bettmann/Corbis; p. 26 Hulton/Archive; p. 28 Corbis; pp. 32, 34 Hulton/Archive; p. 36 David Muench/Corbis; pp. 37, 39, 40 Bettmann/Corbis.

PUBLISHER'S NOTE: This story is based on the author's extensive research, which he/she believes to be accurate. Some parts of the text might have been created by the author based on his/her research to illustrate what might have happened years ago, and is solely an aid to readability for young adults.

    The spelling of the names in this book follow the generally accepted usage of modern day. The spelling of Spanish names in English has evolved over time with no consistency. Many names have been anglicized and no longer use the accent marks or any Spanish grammar. Others have retained the Spanish grammar. Hence, we refer to Hernando de Soto as "de Soto," but Francisco Vásquez de Coronado as "Coronado." There are other variances as well. Some sources might spell Vásquez as Vazquez. For the most part, we have adapted the more widely recognized spellings.

CONTENTS

The Texas defenders of the Alamo fighting the Mexican soldiers within the walls of the fortress. Davy Crockett (shown in center with the gun above his head) died in the siege. The most famous battle of the Texas war for independence from Mexico was fought in March 1836 at the old mission San Antonio de Valero, commonly called the Alamo, which had been turned into a fortress.

REMEMBER THE ALAMO!

CHAPTER 1

The Revolutionary War is without question America's most famous war of independence. But there was another war for freedom fought in Texas about 60 years later that some might argue was just as important in helping shape the United States as we know it today.

Although we now take it for granted that America goes "from sea to shining sea," for many years other countries controlled large regions of North America. By 1783 the 13 British colonies had gained independence from England, but France still controlled the central region, and Spain controlled Florida and Texas and everything west of the Rockies. Driven by the principal of Manifest Destiny, which is the belief that the westward expansion to the Pacific by the United States was inevitable and necessary, America was willing to gain land by any means, whether through sale or use of force.

In 1803 the United States bought the huge Louisiana Territory from France for $15 million. With that one transaction, the United States doubled in size and overnight became one of the largest nations in the world. The Louisiana Territory extended from the Canadian border to the Gulf of Mexico and from the Mississippi River to the Rocky Mountains, making it the single largest land purchase in American history. The purchase of Louisiana not only ended the threat of war with France but opened up the land west of the Mississippi to settlement. The acquisition of California was less amicable, and in the 1840s resulted in the U.S.-Mexico War, which was fought over an area that now includes Utah, New Mexico, Arizona, Nevada, Colorado, and California.

However, the seeds of that conflict had actually been sown more than 10 years earlier in Texas. There, people had become increasingly unhappy with being ruled by Mexico and wanted to govern themselves. The leaders of Mexico, however, were unwilling to give Texans their freedom. Tensions between the two groups continued to grow and eventually led to the Texas War of Independence.

Ironically, Mexico itself was a newly independent country. Like much of North America, Mexico had originally been claimed by Spain through a number of Spanish explorers and adventurers. In 1519, Alonzo Álvarez de Pineda became the first known European to explore and map the Texas coastline. Nine years later Álvar Núñez Cabeza de Vaca was shipwrecked, reportedly on Galveston Island off the Texas coast, and eventually explored the Texas interior on his way to Mexico.

Between 1540 and 1542, Francisco Vásquez de Coronado led an expedition of over 300 soldiers across northern Texas in search of the so-called Seven Cities of Cibola. According to Spanish legend, many years earlier seven bishops and their congregations had sailed west and founded seven cities of gold in the New World. However, Coronado was never able to find the cities. Since then, historians have speculated that the legend was rooted in an optical illusion. When viewed from a distance, the straw that was used to make adobe bricks could have glittered in the sunlight and taken on a golden appearance.

Throughout the 1700s, Spain cemented its presence in Mexico, of which Texas was a part, by establishing Catholic missions in a number of Texas cities, including Goliad, Nacogdoches, and San Antonio. But the seeds of revolution were sown in Mexico on September 16, 1810, when a Catholic priest named Miguel Hidalgo y Costilla in the village of Dolores, Guanajuato, ordered the arrest of the Spaniards who lived in Dolores. He then rang the church bell to summon all the townspeople. Urging them to take up arms against Spain, he shouted out, *Viva México!* Eleven years later, in 1821, Mexico won its independence. However, it was reluctant to give Texans the same freedom, and the stage was set for war.

The most famous battle of that war was fought in March 1836 at the old mission San Antonio de Valero, commonly called the Alamo, which had been turned into a fortress. After losing San Antonio (then called Bexar by the Mexicans) to the Texans during the Siege of Bexar, a Mexican general named Antonio López de Santa Anna was determined to win back this key location. He also wanted to flex the might of the Mexican army in hopes of extinguishing Texas opposition to Mexican rule.

As the Mexican forces streamed into San Antonio, about 150 Texans and American volunteers, which included frontiersman Davy Crockett, took refuge in the Alamo, under the joint command of Lieutenant Colonel William B. Travis and Jim Bowie. Eventually over 2,000 Mexican soldiers surrounded the Alamo, but the men inside refused to surrender, even though they knew they would never get out alive. Knowing he was facing an impossible situation, Travis wrote the now famous Appeal for Aid that many people believe symbolizes the bravery and character of the American people:

In March 1836, Santa Anna and his Mexican soldiers defeated the 187 Texas soldiers at the Alamo. A month later at the Battle of San Jacinto, the Texas battle cry became, "Remember the Alamo!" It was Santa Anna's wish that the few survivors retell the story of the Alamo so that they would not continue to oppose Mexico. Instead, "Remember the Alamo" became their rallying cry.

Colonel William Travis offers an escape to his troops before the Battle of the Alamo, but none defect.

"I am besieged, by a thousand or more of the Mexicans under Santa Anna. . . . The enemy has demanded surrender . . . otherwise, the garrison are to be put to the sword, if the fort is taken. I have answered the demand with a cannon shot, & our flag still waves proudly from the walls. I shall never surrender or retreat. Then, I call on you in the name of Liberty, of patriotism & everything dear to the American character, to come to our aid, with all dispatch. The enemy is receiving reinforcements daily and will no doubt increase to three or four thousand in four or five days. If this call is neglected, I am determined to sustain myself as long as possible and die like a soldier who never forgets what is due to his own honor and that of his country—Victory or Death."

The Texans and Americans holed up in the Alamo were able to hold off Santa Anna's army for two weeks. But on the morning of March 6, the Mexicans stormed the fortress and killed nearly all the defenders. Only a few lives were spared, including those of Susanna Dickinson, the wife of one of the defenders, and their baby. It was Santa Anna's desire that the few survivors tell the story of the Alamo defeat to prevent others from continuing their opposition to Mexico. Instead, *Remember the Alamo!* became just as much of a rallying cry for Texans as *Viva México* had been for Mexicans in their war against Spain.

Guns blaze from the windows of the Alamo where the Texas defenders held off Santa Anna and his troops for 13 days before being defeated.

Just as George Washington, Benjamin Franklin, and Thomas Jefferson are forever remembered as founders of our country, the Texas War of Independence also had its heroes. These people were instrumental in winning Texas's independence from Mexico and its subsequent statehood. Among those who carried on the fight for freedom in the name of those who gave their lives at the Alamo was a Mexican-born Texan named Lorenzo de Zavala. Although Zavala may not be as familiar to most people as Sam Houston and Stephen Austin are, his vision and contributions to the state of Texas have forever earned him a place of honor and importance in American history.■

The Alamo still stands today in downtown San Antonio.

Lorenzo De Zavala was an important player in the Texas quest for independence, but his name is little known outside the Texan border.

AN ACTIVIST IS BORN

Lorenzo de Zavala, whose full name was Manuel Lorenzo Justiniano de Zavala y Sáenz, was born on October 3, 1788, in the village of Tecoh, near what is now the city of Mérida, Yucatán, just inland from the Gulf of Mexico on the tip of the Yucatán peninsula. Lorenzo was the fifth of nine children born to Anastasio de Zavala y Velázquez and María Bárbara Sáenz y Castro.

Lorenzo's childhood was uneventful and typical for the times. By the late 1700s, Mexico, which was part of the vast region known as New Spain, or *Nueva España*, had developed its own unique culture, and the people who had been born there thought of themselves as Mexicans, not Spaniards.

Like many Mexicans, the Zavala family was Catholic. So were many of the indigenous, or native, Indians, who had been converted by the flood of missionaries who had come to the New World when the area was first settled. Even though native Indians learned Spanish and adopted European ways and fashions, they were still considered second-class citizens—as were the mestizos, the people of mixed Indian, European, and sometimes black descent—because the society in New Spain was based on the authority of European-born Spaniards. Even criollos, people of pure Spanish descent who were born in the Americas, were considered beneath Spaniards born in Europe. As a result, there was a huge imbalance in educational and financial opportunities between the social classes.

Not everyone agreed with this kind of government-approved discrimination. These inequalities caused many people in Mexico to resent the Spanish authorities and fed their growing desire for independence.

It was against this backdrop of increasing social upheaval that Lorenzo grew up. His parents, who believed in equality for all people, raised their son to be an open-minded thinker and to respect all people. Lorenzo also enjoyed the advantages of a good education, which further reinforced those beliefs. In 1807, when he was 19, Lorenzo graduated from the Tridentine Seminary of San Ildefonso in Mérida, where he had taken classes such as philosophy and moral theology. That same year, despite his youth, he also married Teresa Correa y Correa; they looked forward to starting a family of their own.

After he left the seminary, he founded the first newspaper published in Yucatán, and he would later publish others. In addition to writing for the paper, he also acted as the editor. He used his publication to express his strong political views, which stressed democratic ideals, such as people's individual rights. These views would later become the foundation for his lifelong political activism.

Through his work at the paper and the editorials he wrote, Lorenzo earned the respect of many people, who urged him to pursue a career in politics. At that time Mexico was in a state of upheaval. When the Bourbon family had come to power in Spain in the 1700s, they made many changes that angered the people of New Spain. They removed all criollos and Mexican-based Spaniards from positions of authority, sending officials from Europe to govern in their place. They also promoted heavier taxes and increased the size of the army, which added further unrest in New Spain. The monarchy of Spain, which at one point in history was looked on with reverence and awe by the people of New Spain, was increasingly seen as unjust and an obstacle to personal freedom.

In 1810, the criollos, supported by the Indians and mestizos, had started the revolution for independence. Spain fought back by cracking down on those who spoke out against the government. Zavala could think of nothing he would rather do more, so from 1812 to 1814 he served as the secretary of the Mérida city council, all the while continuing to speak out on behalf of democracy and supporting the idea of an independent Mexico. He criticized the government's attempts to curb free speech and to censor, or restrict, the press.

However, Zavala would soon learn that not everybody agreed with his positions—especially the Spanish government officials. His political activism resulted in his being arrested and sent to jail at the San Juan de Ulloa prison for advocating democratic reforms in the Spanish government. The prison was located on an island off the Mexican coast at Veracruz. It had been built in the 1500s as a fortress to protect the area against pirates. Later turned into a prison for mostly political prisoners, it became notorious for the brutal way some inmates were treated in the prison's sinister dungeons.

This is the moat that surrounds Castillo de San Juan de Ulloa in Veracruz, Mexico. It was built in the 1500s as a fortress to protect the area from pirates, but the Spanish government used it as a prison. Zavala was imprisoned here when he criticized the government's attempts to curb free speech.

Luckily, Zavala managed to avoid any excessive brutality. He used his time there as productively as he could. Already able to speak Latin and French, he taught himself English and soon became fluent. He also studied medical textbooks made available to him in prison and amazingly taught himself how to be a doctor. Zavala was so skilled in medicine that upon his release from prison in 1817, he decided to give up his political career and practice medicine instead. Not only was he helping people and earning a comfortable living, it was a lot safer than being a political activist during a revolution.

For the next two years, Lorenzo de Zavala lived quietly with his wife and their three children. He spent his days taking care of the sick and staying out of trouble with the authorities. But it wasn't in his nature to just sit back and not be involved. In 1819 he ended his self-imposed exile and got back into politics. Zavala was elected to public office in 1820, and a year later New Spain finally won its independence and officially changed its name to Mexico. Interestingly, though, Mexico's ties to Spain remained strong; in 1821 Zavala was appointed deputy to the Spanish *cortes*, or parliament.

Zavala was a leader of the Federalist Party, which believed in a strong national government, and he looked forward to helping Mexico establish itself. But little could he imagine that his days of being a revolutionary were far from over. ■

SIMMS LIBRARY
ALBUQUERQUE ACADEMY

A portrait of Antonio López de Santa Anna (1795-1876). Santa Anna was born in Jalapa, in the province of Veracruz on February 21, 1795. At the age of 15, he became a cadet in the Spanish Army stationed in Mexico and began his long career by fighting against the Mexicans in the War of Independence. He ruled Mexico as President 11 times during the 1800s, but he was overthrown each time.

SHATTERED DREAMS

W hen Zavala returned to Mexico from Spain, he became one of the early leaders of the new country whose goal was to establish a republican government. Because of his passion for justice and keen intelligence, his political career flourished. In 1822 and again in 1824, the year the Mexican Constitution was written, Zavala was elected to the Mexican Congress. Like most Mexicans, Zavala looked to the future with optimism. He believed his country was on its way to fulfilling the democratic ideals so important to him.

Patterned somewhat after the Constitution of the United States, the Mexican version established a Congress to oversee laws, made the Catholic Church the official religion, promised to support the church through taxes, and provided for a president and vice president to be elected to four-year terms. However, instead of the people of Mexico choosing the president, the Congress of each state would decide. Each state was allowed to make its own laws, as long as they didn't contradict the Constitution, and to elect its own officials.

In 1825 Zavala was elected to the Mexican Senate; he served as a senator until 1826. Then in 1827 he became governor of the state of Mexico. There were many who believed that he might one day be elected president of all Mexico. And Zavala indeed seemed to be positioning himself for such leadership. However, his fortunes would soon take an unexpected turn.

Like many other Mexicans of high rank, Zavala was a member of the Freemasons, which is one of the world's oldest fraternities. The word *fraternity* comes from the Latin word for "brother" and means "a formal group of likeminded individuals." The Freemasons, also called Masons, trace their roots back to the medieval trade guilds of stonemasons, but the modern organization was officially founded in London in 1717. It quickly spread across Europe and then on to the American colonies. Different areas have individual clubs, called lodges. Its structure is similar to that of the YMCA, which is one organization made up of clubs around the world. Today, there is an estimated 6 million Freemasons—all of whom are men. Women are not allowed to join.

The goal of the Masons is to "teach a man the duty he owes to God, his neighbor, and himself." The three great principles, or ideals, of the Masons are brotherly love (Masons will show tolerance and respect for the opinions of others), charity, and truth. Although Freemasonry is not affiliated with any specific religion or belief, members are required to believe in God.

It is easy to see what appealed to Zavala about the Masons, because he obviously shared their belief about truth, charity, and respecting one's fellows. In 1826 the Grand

Lodge of New York issued charters for five lodges in Mexico City. After joining the Masons, Lorenzo soon became a leader within the group. Interestingly, Masons are nonpolitical and today discussions of any political nature are forbidden at the lodges. But during Zavala's time, that wasn't always the case. Zavala became the Charter Master of *Independencia* Lodge No. 454, which, like the other four Mexican Mason lodges, was made up of men who favored a constitutional democracy. The other main political view in Mexico at the time was Centralist. Centralists supported an autocratic government under a monarch or dictator. Because of this conflict, the Masons were seen by some as a political force and were regarded with suspicion.

By 1828, political infighting and the inability of Mexico to establish a stable government had thrown the country into turmoil. In the election held in September, the state legislatures voted Manuel Gómez Pedraza to be president. However, the followers of General Vicente Guerrero, including the powerful General Antonio Santa Anna, rejected the vote, and revolts and protests broke out all over Mexico. Pedraza eventually was forced to flee the presidency on December 3, 1828, when his troops couldn't end the revolt. As a result, the Mexican Congress gave the presidency to Guerrero in April 1829.

The northernmost Mexican states, including Texas, dreamed of being independent states within a Mexican Republic, precisely the same vision Zavala had. For a while, the election of General Guerrero, who had been a major figure in Mexico's fight for independence, gave hope to the Federalists that the dream might still come true. However, there were many in Mexico who were worried about the growing strength of Texas and were determined not to give it and other Mexican states too much freedom.

President Guerrero was a good friend of Zavala's. Zavala served in Guerrero's administration as minister of the treasury after turning down the opportunity to go to Washington, D.C., as ambassador to the United States. In exchange for his loyalty and service to his country, Zavala obtained a land grant in East Texas on March 12, 1829. He was going to use the land to settle five hundred families. But his position as minister of the treasury prevented him from devoting the necessary time to the colonization project.

There were other problems facing Zavala as well. His political enemies began to criticize his performance, and when he returned to his native state of Yucatán in December 1829, he was greeted with cold contempt by the locals, who did not want to give Texas its independence.

More ominous for Zavala were the political ambitions of Mexican General Santa Anna, who was determined to take control of the government. To that end, he assisted Guerrero's vice president, Centralist Anastasio Bustamante, stage a coup d'état, which is when a government is taken over by force. Most coups, as they are generally called, are done with the support of the military and/or police. Coups still happen today, usually in countries with so much political strife that the people offer little resistance to the breakdown of law.

After Guerrero was deposed, or forced out of office, he was tracked down by the new president's army and eventually executed, so he in turn could not try to stage his own coup d'état. But Bustamante didn't realize his biggest enemy was the same man who had helped him take over the presidency. Just two years later, Santa Anna staged yet another coup and replaced Bustamante with Pedraza, who had won the 1828 election in the first place and had been in exile in the United States since fleeing Mexico.

But Pedraza held the presidency for only a few months, because his term was nearly over. In the next elections, Santa Anna ran and was elected president.

After Guerrero was forced from office, Zavala was kept under house arrest by the new government and then forced into exile in 1830. He went to New York City in October of that year and transferred his interest in his land grants to the Galveston Bay and Texas Land Company. After spending several months during 1831 in France and England, Zavala came back to New York. In the summer of 1832, he once again heeded the call of his country.

After Santa Anna assumed the presidency, he appointed Zavala Mexican minister to France. While in Paris, however, after Santa Anna named himself dictator, it became clear to Zavala that Santa Anna had no intention of ever upholding the Mexican Constitution. Disappointed and disillusioned, Zavala resigned in protest, left France, and sailed to New York, believing his political career was finally over.

Little did he know, his greatest triumphs lay ahead. ■

Stephen Fuller Austin (1793-1836) was a famous colonizer of Texas. He served as Secretary of State of the Republic of Texas. In 1835, Austin had assumed temporary command of the Texas army during the revolution and Lorenzo de Zavala quickly won his trust. He was so influential that anytime Austin had to leave on business, Zavala assumed leadership. Austin also incorporated many of Zavala's ideas into his own political writings.

A NEW BEGINNING

Because Santa Anna had effectively dismantled the Mexican Constitution, Zavala could no longer live in Mexico and support the government. Although he had become president after a democratic election, Santa Anna decided that Mexico wasn't prepared to handle democracy, so he named himself dictator, assuming complete control over the government. This was not only bad news for Zavala, it was also a terrible turn of events for all Texans, because Santa Anna had no intention of giving Texas the freedom to govern itself. As a result, Antonio López de Santa Anna became a villain in the eyes of all Texans.

Throughout his life, Santa Anna displayed the manipulative and self-centered qualities that would eventually lead to his repeatedly gaining and losing power. Santa Anna was born in the state of Veracruz in 1795 and entered the army as a cadet when he was just 16. His tendency to switch sides was first seen when he initially fought for the Spanish against Mexican independence, but then abruptly turned against Spain in 1821, right before Mexico's victory. Despite this, he continued to rise through the ranks and earned the title of general when he was just 27 years old.

After he helped Guerrero assume the presidency, Santa Anna was rewarded by being appointed the highest-ranking general in Mexico. Because he was instrumental in helping defeat Spain's attempt to reclaim Mexico in 1829, it wasn't surprising that Santa Anna was overwhelmingly elected president of Mexico. Unfortunately for the Mexican people in general and Texans in particular, Santa Anna's promise to unite the new nation wasn't kept. Through it all, he showed no remorse.

Santa Anna on horseback with two of his aides.

"It is very true that I threw up my cap for liberty with great ardor, and perfect sincerity, but very soon found the folly of it," he would write years later. "A hundred years to come my people will not be fit for liberty. They do not know what it is, unenlightened as they are, and under the influence of a Catholic clergy, a despotism is the proper government for them, but there is no reason why it should not be a wise and virtuous one."

In the end, striking down the Mexican Constitution was the final straw for many Texans and provided the spark for revolution. Both the American colonists in Texas and Mexicans living in the region were equally convinced that their lives would be better off free from Mexican rule.

During his two-year exile from Mexico, from 1830 to 1832, Zavala's life seemed to be a series of tragedies. First, he had been driven from his native country. Then, in the spring of 1831, Teresa died. However, Lorenzo did not stay a widower for long. Later that year, in November, he married 22-year-old Emily West, an American who had been born in Rensselaer, New York. They would eventually also have three children, a daughter and two sons.

After resigning his post in France to protest Santa Anna, Zavala had good reason to be fearful for his life, so he moved his family to Texas, where he had bought land a year earlier. During this time, he wrote in his diary: "Is a man, I would ask, who has invited these trusts from his fellow citizens a vagrant and a wicked man? I have been President of the general Congress and my name stands first in the Constitution of Mexico. I have been president of the Senate and today I am a Colonist of the Province of Texas."

Lorenzo and Emily settled on a piece of land north of Buffalo Bayou called Zavala Point, near what is now Houston. Interestingly, Emily's "city ways" were reportedly not popular in the neighborhood, which was made up mostly of hard-edged settlers who had not grown up with the finer things in life. But this was now their home, and soon Lorenzo found himself wrapped up in local politics again. This time, though, he took up the cause of Mexican Federalism in opposition to Santa Anna.

By this time Zavala was well known and respected not only for his political service but for his writings as well. Throughout his exile he had published a number of pamphlets, memorials, and books. The books he is best remembered for are a two-volume history of Mexico, *Ensayo histórico de las revoluciones de México desde 1808 hasta 1830* and *Viage a los Estados-Unidos del Norte de América*, in which he described what it was like in the United States during his time there between 1830 and 1832.

In 1835, Texas officially revolted against Mexico, and Zavala quickly won the trust of leaders such as Stephen Austin, who had assumed temporary command of the Texas Army during the revolution. Because of his experience with the Mexican government, Zavala was an invaluable resource. He was so influential that anytime Austin had to leave on business, Zavala assumed leadership. Austin also incorporated many of Zavala's ideas into his own political writings.

Throughout this time, Zavala was considered a fugitive by Santa Anna, and in fact there were standing orders to arrest him and send him to southern Mexico. However, Lorenzo was safe in Texas, where he was frequently invited to attend political meetings.

His political experience was also crucial during the Consultation of 1835, a meeting of representatives of various districts of Texas that took place in Columbia. The purpose of the Consultation was to discuss the escalating tensions with Mexico and to decide what options the Texans had.

However, by the date the Consultation was scheduled to begin, October 16, fighting had already broken out between Mexican and Texas forces. The meeting was quickly adjourned, or called off. On October 31, Zavala wrote an article for the *Telegraph and Texas Register* in which he urged the Mexican population of Texas to support the revolution.

The Consultation reconvened, or got back together, on November 4 in San Felipe. Not surprisingly, there was a lot of disagreement among the members as to what the best course of action would be. There were three main lines: There were those who supported Austin and favored trying to gain the support of Mexican liberals. Another group was more anti-Mexican, and the third group tried to find a compromise between the other two groups.

Even though there was a lot of discussion about compromising with Mexico, most who participated, including Zavala, clearly wanted a much more independent Texas. Many others wanted the state to remain part of the Mexican Republic. The Consultation stopped short of declaring independence from Mexico, although the members made it clear they had the right to do so if it chose. The participants voted 33 to 14 in favor of establishing a provisional government, with Henry Smith as governor. After the Consultation drafted its declaration, the members asked Zavala to translate it into Spanish.

However, the Consultation failed to establish a clear power structure, so when the meeting ended, Texas was still without the strong leadership it needed. That would soon change. ■

Sam Houston (1793-1863) was an American soldier and politician. A former U. S. Congressman and governor of Tennessee who happened to be a close friend of President Andrew Jackson, Houston was an influential delegate seeking support from the United States for the Texas cause for freedom. He was chosen commander in chief of the revolutionary army and he left the convention early to take charge of the forces gathering at the city of Gonzales. The city of Houston, Texas is named for him.

TURNING THE TIDE

After the Consultation, representatives from Texas went to the United States seeking support for the Texas cause. However, the message was clear: America wouldn't offer support as long as Texas continued to pledge loyalty to the Mexican Constitution. In other words, if Texans wanted help, they had to pledge their allegiance to the United States over Mexico.

On March 1, 1836, forty-four delegates from all over Texas representing the 17 settlements met at Washington-on-the-Brazos, 70 miles northwest of Houston. It was immediately obvious that the mood among the people of Texas had changed and that outright independence was now favored by a majority. The delegates knew they must declare independence or submit to Mexican authority. But in choosing independence, it was vital to draft a constitution for their new nation, to establish a strong provisional government, and to prepare to fight Santa Anna. His armies had already invaded Texas and at that very moment had the Alamo surrounded.

The makeup of the delegates said a lot about the melting-pot nature of Texas. Two-thirds were under 40 years old. Two were native Texans, Zavala was a native Mexican, and the majority were American settlers. Most had been in Texas less than a year. But all were dedicated to freedom. Although Zavala had originally favored an independent Texas that remained part of Mexico, he know realized his Mexican countrymen were not going to drive Santa Anna from power, so the only recourse was for Texas to be truly independent.

Andrew Jackson (1767-1845) was President of the United States from 1829 to 1837, during which time Texas was fighting for its independence. Sam Houston was a close friend of Jackson's and a supporter of Texas independence.

One of the more influential delegates was Sam Houston, who was a former U.S. congressman and governor of Tennessee and who happened to be a close friend of U.S. President Andrew Jackson. Houston was chosen commander in chief of the revolutionary army; he left the convention early to take charge of the forces gathering at the city of Gonzales.

George C. Childress was appointed to head a committee of five men to draft a declaration of independence. When the committee met that evening, Childress drew from his pocket a document that followed the outline and main features of the U.S. Declaration of Independence. The next day, on March 2, the delegates unanimously adopted the Texas Declaration of Independence, which created the Republic of Texas. They quickly prepared a constitution, again fashioned after the United States', and formed an interim government, which would serve until October 1836, when general elections could be held. David G. Burnet was named interim president, and Zavala was his vice president.

By signing the Texas Declaration of Independence, Zavala became one of Texas's founding fathers. At the same time, however, to many Mexicans he became a traitor to his own country. Zavala followed his heart and his beliefs, all the while knowing it meant he was permanently cutting ties with his native land.

One of the last things the convention did was to declare all able-bodied men between the ages of 17 and 50 fit for military service. In return, the soldiers would be given land, from 320 to 1,280 acres for service of from three months to one year. Those men who left Texas to avoid military service, refused to participate, or in any way gave aid to the enemy would forfeit their rights of citizenship and any land they owned.

But few refused the call to arms, especially after the Alamo. News of the bravery of the men who defended the Alamo against Santa Anna quickly spread across the land, adding fuel to the revolutionary fire already burning in most Texans. The battle of the Alamo was important for another reason—because the men defending the Alamo were able to hold off Santa Anna for so long and killed so many of his soldiers, it gave other Texans time to regroup and prepare.

After the convention, Zavala rejoined his family at their home on Buffalo Bayou. But just a few weeks later, they had to run for their lives. Santa Anna's troops had orders to capture Zavala and others who were fighting against Mexico.

The Zavala family fled down the San Jacinto River to the home of William Scott. The area is preserved today as the San Jacinto Battleground State Historic Park.

The Zavala family fled down the San Jacinto River to the home of William Scott, a close friend of Stephen Austin's. At one point Emily tried to go back to their house to retrieve a chest of silverware, but she had to turn back as the army was closing in fast. Along with a number of other families, the Zavalas boarded a steamship that took them to safety on Galveston Island. There they awaited word on the outcome of what would be the decisive battle of the war.

On April 19, 1836, Sam Houston led a small army of Texans to where the Buffalo Bayou and the San Jacinto River meet. They dug in between a protective grove of trees and an open field. There they waited for Santa Anna. Although the troops were getting impatient, Houston was cautious. He knew he could make no mistake.

This painting by S. Seymour Thomas hangs in the San Jacinto Museum. It shows General Sam Houston on horseback at the Battle of San Jacinto.

Even during his life, Houston was considered one of the more colorful characters in Texas. He had been born in Virginia and had grown up in Tennessee, where he befriended the local Cherokee Indians. He joined the army and earned the rank of first lieutenant before resigning in 1818 to study law. He practiced law for a short time but was drawn to politics. He served in Congress and as governor of Tennessee.

When his term was over, he went back and spent time with the Cherokees until 1832, when he decided to move to Texas with some friends. Once there, Houston got back into politics and quickly became a recognized leader. After being put in charge of the Texas Army, he ordered the troops to retreat so that they could regroup. He then led them to San Jacinto, where he would wait for Santa Anna.

The Mexican forces arrived on April 20. Houston surprised them with a cannon volley, forcing Santa Anna to seek shelter behind a clump of trees. The Texas cavalry took the opportunity to charge the Mexicans, but the battle was short-lived. Although the skirmish succeeded in firing up the Texans, Santa Anna's army was confident. There were 1,500 of them and only 750 Texans, and thanks to victories at the Alamo and other battles, they believed they would defeat the Texans with ease.

Early on the morning of April 21, Houston sent a few men to destroy the bridge over which the Mexican army had passed, cutting off their only available escape. Once that was done, he gave the order to advance. Everywhere you could hear the shouts of "Remember the Alamo!" as the Texans raced forward, guns blasting. Within a very short time, 700 Mexicans had been killed and 730 taken prisoner, including the proud Santa Anna. Just like that, the Battle of San Jacinto was over, and the battle for Texas was, for all intents and purposes, won. ■

The San Jacinto Monument near Channelview honors the Texans who fought in the Battle of San Jacinto. It marks the site of the 1836 battle in which Texas forces defeated Santa Anna's Mexican army and won independence.

A captive Santa Anna is brought before General Sam Houston on April 22, 1836, the day after the great Texas victory at San Jacinto. After his victory at the Alamo, Santa Anna was confident he could beat the Texans again; however, his army was routed and he was taken prisoner. The Texans forced him to sign a treaty acknowledging the independence of Texas. But the treaty was rejected in Mexico and Santa Anna was removed from power.

CHAPTER 6

A NEW REPUBLIC

lthough being elected vice president had been one of the greatest honors in his life, it was not an easy position, and Zavala frequently found himself at odds with President Burnet. On April 22, citing his desire to assist the new government in a more active capacity, Zavala resigned. A week later he met with Santa Anna, who was being held prisoner, during the treaty negotiations. For several weeks Zavala acted as both interpreter and liaison, or go-between, for Santa Anna and the Texas government. Two weeks after negotiations were concluded on May 14, Zavala was appointed to accompany Santa Anna to Mexico to negotiate a treaty that would officially recognize the Texas Republic.

Once again, Zavala agreed to take the position of vice president, and once again he had a change of heart. He resigned for the second time on June 3, after President Burnet gave in to those in the army and new government who wanted Santa Anna executed for the slaughter at the Alamo. Zavala condemned the action, noting that "a government that takes orders from armed masses is no longer a body politic." In another show of protest, he helped Santa Anna compose a letter to Burnet denouncing his treatment.

The experience prompted Zavala to adopt a new position. He felt he had fulfilled all his obligations to Texas, and now he believed it was in the Republic's best interest to become part of the United States. He wrote to a friend, "for by this action the stability of our government will be assured and because I believe it will be very difficult for Texas to march alone among the other independent nations."

Lorenzo de Zavala and his family finally returned to their Buffalo Bayou home in June and discovered their house had been used as a makeshift hospital in the aftermath of the battle. Although still a young man, Lorenzo's health was fragile, and throughout the rest of the summer he suffered from recurrent bouts of malaria.

On September 11 he wrote an associate a letter saying that he expected to be strong enough to attend the opening session of the government, but two weeks later he was still too sick to travel. On October 14, President Burnet wrote Zavala suggesting that both he and Zavala resign so that the newly elected government, to be led by president-elect Sam Houston, could be inaugurated at once. Zavala submitted his third and final resignation, dated October 17, 1836, and marked the official end of his political career.

Less than a month later, Zavala was on the Buffalo Bayou in a rowboat during a storm. The rowboat overturned, sending him into the freezing cold water. He developed pneumonia, and over the next month his health declined rapidly. He died on November 15, 1836, and was buried in a small cemetery plot on his property. The plot has since sunk into Buffalo Bayou.

After Lorenzo de Zavala died, Emily moved back to New York City. She remarried and returned with her new husband to Zavala Point in early 1839. There they raised two children. Emily would be widowed twice more but continued to live on Buffalo Bayou until the house burned down in 1866. She later moved to Galveston to be near her eldest son, Augustine, and sold the land at Zavala Point to her second son, Richard, in order to keep the family cemetery in the family. Emily died on June 15, 1882, in Houston and was also buried at Zavala Point.

Although Zavala's name has become somewhat obscure outside the Texas border, those who knew him were aware of his contribution. In his inaugural address Vice President Mirabeau B. Lamar eulogized Zavala, saying,

"Gentlemen, I should be doing an injustice to my own feelings if I were to resume my seat, without paying to my predecessor in office that tribute of respect to which he is justly entitled by his public as well as his private virtues.

"Through a period of a long life the ex-vice president, Governor Lorenzo de Zavala, has been the unwavering and consistent friend of liberal principles of free government. Among the first movers of the revolution he has never departed from the pure and sacred principles upon which it was originally founded. This steady and unyielding devotion to the holy sacred cause of liberty has been amply rewarded by the confidence, of the virtuous portion of two republics. The gentleman, the scholar and the patriot, he goes into retirement with the undivided affections of his fellow citizens; and I know, gentlemen, that I do not express only my own feelings when I say that it is the wish of every member of this assembly that the evening of his day may be as tranquil and happy as the meridian of his life has been useful and honorable; a gentleman, a patriot, a scholar and one who loves his fellow man."

Although he did not live to see it, Texas followed the path Lorenzo de Zavala envisioned and in 1845 became the 28th state of the Union.

CHRONOLOGY

1788   Born in Tecoh, in the state of Yucatán, Mexico, on October 3

1807   Graduates from Tridentine Seminary; marries Teresa Correa y Correa

1814   Sent to prison for three years because of his political views

1817   Works as a medical doctor

1819   Returns to politics

1820   Travels to Madrid as a representative of Yucatán

1821   Returns to Mexico after it wins independence from Spain

1822, 1824   Serves in Mexican Congress

1825–1826   Serves in Mexican Senate

1827   Elected governor of the state of Mexico

1829   Serves under Guerrero as minister of the treasury; granted a contract to introduce five hundred families into Texas

1830   Forced into exile

1831   Teresa dies; Lorenzo marries Emily West

1832   Appointed as Mexican minister to France by President Santa Anna but soon resigns; moves his family to Texas, where he actively supports Mexican Federalism in opposition to Santa Anna

1835   Participates in Consultation of 1835

1836   Signs the Texas Declaration of Independence; is elected vice president of the interim government of the Republic of Texas; family flees Buffalo Bayou; resigns as vice president in October; dies of pneumonia November 15

TIMELINE IN HISTORY

1528   After being shipwrecked, Álvar Núñez Cabeza de Vaca becomes first European to explore Texas.

1540   The Coronado expedition sets out for Texas, the first of what will be 20 Spanish explorations of the area.

1690   The Mission San Francisco de los Tejas is founded.

1694   After Spanish explorer Gregorio de Salinas Varona declares Texas unsuitable for settlement, Spain abandons the area for almost 20 years.

1716   Spain builds a presidio west of the Neches River, marking the beginning of settlement of Texas.

1718   The Mission San Antonio de Valero, better known as the Alamo, is founded.

1821   Mexico wins independence from Spain; the Mexican government gives Moses Austin permission to settle three hundred families in Texas, but Austin dies before he can start his settlement.

1822   Settler Jared Groce brings cotton to Texas.

1830   Mexico passes a law banning American immigration to Texas.

1833   Santa Anna becomes president of Mexico and claims himself dictator.

1834   Stephen Austin is arrested for attempting to start a revolt against Mexico.

1835   The Texas Revolution begins at Gonzales.

1836   The Alamo falls to Santa Anna, among those killed is Davy Crockett; the Texas Declaration of Independence is adopted in March; the Battle of San Jacinto is fought on April 21; Santa Anna and President David Burnet sign the Treaty of Velasco on May 14, making Texas a Republic; Lorenzo de Zavala dies on November 15.

1845   Texas becomes the 28th state.

FOR FURTHER READING

Estep, Raymond. *The Life of Lorenzo de Zavala.* (Ph.D. dissertation, University of Texas, 1942).

———. "Lorenzo de Zavala and the Texas Revolution." *Southwestern Historical Quarterly,* vol. 57, January 1954.

Garland, Sherry, & Ronald Himler (illustrator). *Voices of the Alamo.* New York: Scholastic Trade, 2000.

Henson, Margaret Swett. *Lorenzo de Zavala, the Pragmatic Idealist.* Fort Worth: Texas Christian University Press, 1996.

Venable, Faye. *Lorenzo de Zavala: North to the Rio Grande.* Austin, Tex.: Eakin Publications, 1998.

ON THE WEB

Battle of San Jacinto

http://www.lsjunction.com/events/jacinto.htm

The Handbook of Texas Online

http://www.tsha.utexas.edu/handbook/online/articles/view/ZZ/fza5.html

Lee, R. "The History Guy"

http://www.historyguy.com/lorenzo_de_zavala.html

GLOSSARY

Activism (AK-tuh-VIZ-um): Giving direct action to support or oppose one side of a controversial issue.

Colonization (kol-ih-nih-ZAY-shun): The process by which one nation establishes its culture and government in another area of the world, often eclipsing the culture of the area's indigenous people.

Coup d'état (koo-day-TAH): The takeover of a government by a small group, usually aided by the military.

Criollos (kree-oh-YOHS): People of Spanish descent born in Mexico.

Democracy (dih-MOCK-rah-SEE): Government by the people, either directly or through elected representatives; also a form of society that supports equal rights, freedom of speech, and a fair trial and tolerates the views of minorities.

Indigenous (in-DIJ-ih-NUS): People native to a particular land or area.

Interim (IN-tur-um): Temporary. An interim government is one that fills in until formal elections can be held.

Land grants: Large tracts of land given to individuals by the government.

Manifest Destiny: The belief that the westward expansion to the Pacific by the United States was inevitable and necessary.

Mestizos (mess-TEE-zohs): People of mixed American Indian, European, and often black descent.

Mission (MISH-in): Spanish settlement consisting mainly of American Indians as well as priests, soldiers, and craftspeople for the purpose of converting the native people to Catholicism.

New Spain: The Spanish empire in the Americas, which were colonized by Spain in 17th and 18th centuries; also called *Nueva España*.

Presidio (prih-SID-ee-oh): Spanish military post, usually a rectangular enclosure 650 feet long, with buildings placed along the inside of fortified walls.

Pueblo (PWEB-low): In Spanish America, the term for "village" or "town."

Rancho: Large tracts of land given to Mexican citizens intended for raising cattle.

INDEX